TWO-WEEK RESERVE:
NO RENEWAL

DATE DUE

11			

Our Fathers Had Powerful Songs

OUR FATHERS HAD POWERFUL SONGS by Natalia Belting

illustrated by Laszlo Kubinyi

E. P. DUTTON & CO., INC.   NEW YORK

Library of Congress Cataloging in Publication Data

Belting, Natalia Maree, comp.
Our fathers had powerful songs.

SUMMARY: Poems from various American Indian
tribes celebrating the creation and life of man.

1. Indian poetry—Translations into English.
2. American poetry—Translations from Indian
languages. [1. Indian poetry—Collections]
I. Kubinyi, Laszlo, illus.   II. Title.

 PZ197.E3B4   897   73–13968   ISBN 0–525–36485–4

Published simultaneously in Canada by Clarke,
Irwin & Company Limited, Toronto and Vancouver

Designed by Riki Levinson
Printed in the U.S.A.
First Edition

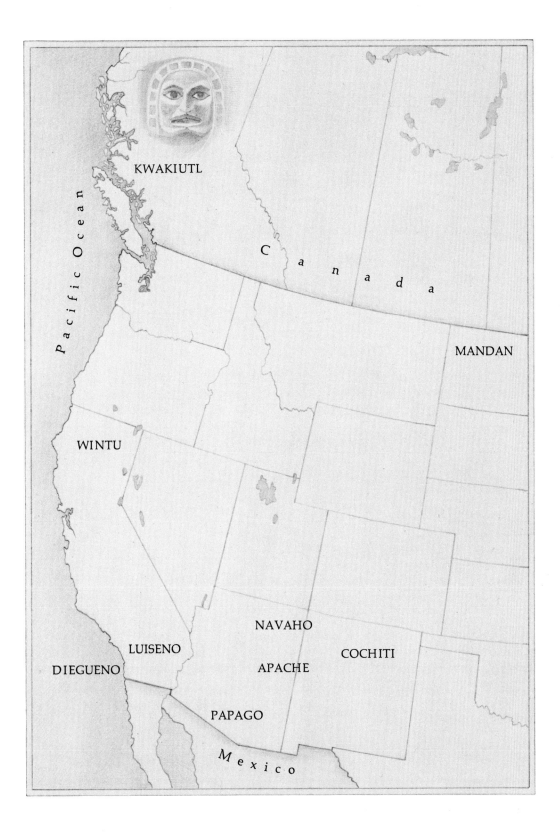

KWAKIUTL

Pacific Ocean

Canada

MANDAN

WINTU

NAVAHO

LUISENO

COCHITI

DIEGUENO

APACHE

PAPAGO

Mexico

Our fathers had powerful songs
In the beginning
When they scattered
To find themselves homes on the earth.

They sang, and the land they stood on
Was theirs; no other men
Owned it. The song made it theirs.

(Turtle sang. The rock where he sang
Was marked like his back by his singing.
The rock became his.)

They sang for water
And it came out in springs,
Flowed in rivers,
Gathered itself in lakes and ponds.

They sang, and their songs
Made the months, and the seasons:

 When Frog hides away and there is no rain,
 When Elk has her young.
 When Bear sheds his coat.
 When Sky's blue color fades.
 When streams wash leaves that have fallen,
 When winter clouds pile up.

They sang, and their songs
Established the dances,
The ceremonial dances:

 The mourning dance,
 The dance of the spirits,
 The women's dance, and the dance of the girls,
 The rain-making dance, and the harvest dance,
 The healing dances, and the dances of blessing.

Our fathers had powerful songs.
In the land of the dead, they still dance,
And sing their ancient magic songs.
We can hear them yet,
The footfalls, and the humming,
Whenever we lie down and put an ear to the earth.

LUISENO
California

LUISENO

The rains began and they did not stop.
They flooded the rivers, the streams;
The lakes ran over.

Water covered the land, rose
Over the mountain forest, drowned
The spruce and the larch and the limber pine,
Washed snow from the mountain peaks.

Frog floated in a basket.
Owl perched on its handle.
Pine Grosbeak and Mudhen
Rode on the rim of it.

Owl sang his magic song,
And the waters began to go down.

Frog sang his song,
Pine Grosbeak sang,
And Mudhen.

The floods drained from the forests,
Rushed down out of the canyons,
Fell off the mesas,
Went off through the creeks and the streams
To the sea

While Frog and Owl,
Pine Grosbeak and Mudhen
Sang.

WINTU
California

Little men live
In the warrior's scalp basket
That hangs on the middle lodge pole.

If they are not fed,
They creep out at night
In enemy dress,
With matted hair
And masks of dirty paint,

Snatch the blankets off the children sleeping,
Whisper evil in the women's ears,

Make sick the men and boys.

Then a singer is sent for,
A handful of cornmeal put in his hand
To invite him.

At sunset he comes in
And sings the songs of the scalp-basket dwarfs.
At the end of each song
He lets the sick one
Breathe his own breath.

He sings until the sun comes up,
Sings against the dwarfs and their power,
Against the power that causes the scalp-basket sickness,
Sings the curing songs.

PAPAGO
Southwest

The women were digging clams.

At low tide the village women
Were out with the digging sticks
For cockles and clams.

Daughter-of-a-Chief
Saw the enemy coming,
Saw their canoes driving to shore.

She threw down her stick.
She looked at the enemy coming,
She sang her magic song:

Sisters-of-the-Sun, the clouds,
Sucked daylight into their blackness.

She sang:

Thunderbird came to the door of his lodge,
Raised his blanket,
Lightning flashed,
Sheared the sky and the water.

She sang:

North Wind emptied hail from his bag,
Filled the canoes with hailstones,
Sank them.

Daughter-of-a-Chief with her magic song
Saved the women.

KWAKIUTL
Northwest Coast

KWAKIUTL

Coyote stood at the edge
Of prairie-dog town.

"I'll make it rain," he said.
"I'll wash them out of their holes. I am
Hungry for prairie-dog meat."

Coyote sang. "Cloud, dark cloud,
Rain cloud,
Rain on prairie-dog town.

"Rain, rain, rain, rain,"
Coyote sang. Four times
He sang his rain-making song.

And it rained, rained all around
The prairie-dog town, to the north,
And the south and the east and the west
It rained. But not
On prairie-dog town.

"Your song is no good,"
The prairie-dogs laughed at Coyote
Slinking away in the rain.

APACHE
Southwest

When a man dies
Songs lift him up
To the land of the spirits,
To the river of stars
Where the First People live.

The death songs are sung
By dancers in skirts
Made of feathers of eagles.

The clothes of the dead
Are burned, and rise in the smoke.

The songs of Tovit, the rabbit,
Are sung, for Rabbit,
When First Man died,

Made the song that carried him
To the land of the dead,
To the river of stars.

LUISENO
California

The gods made man
Of turquoise and white shell,
Striped corn and blue corn,
Red corn and black;

Made his feet of the earth,
His legs and his tongue
From the lightning, his voice
From the thunder;

Made him of pollen
And rain water, lake water,
And mountain spring water;

Made his arms from the rainbow,
His hair from black night,
His face from the dawn sky,

And they named him
Created-from-Everything.

They made him,
Sang over him through the night,
So that breath entered his body,
So that he moved,
So that his feet danced with the wind.

The gods sang,
And man had life.
They gave him songs,
And he had power.

NAVAHO
Southwest

NAVAHO

Quail sings to her children playing
In the grass at the foot of the cliff,
And they dance to the beat of her song.

Duck sings to her children
And they swim in time to her singing.

Quail's song has power,
Keeps Hawk and Coyote away from her chicks.

Duck's song has power,
Keeps her ducklings from being drawn down
In the whirlpool.

COCHITI
Southwest

When the moon comes up in the daytime
Pale and thin
The Sick Moon ceremony is held.

The women cease gathering milkweed for twine,
Cease basket-making, and weaving.

The men put away their long willow bows,
Their quivers and arrows,
Put an end to their hunting,

And they all go down, the whole of the village,
To the stream.

They bathe, and they sport in the water,
Run foot races, joke, and tell tales.

They laugh, and the women sing
Songs to make the moon glad.

Each has her own song and she sings it,
They cure the sick moon with their fun and their songs.

DIEGUENO
California

Sun's boat is a bowl of buffalo-skin,
A bull-hide canoe.
His songs are the paddles.

At daybreak he stands in the door of his lodge
At the edge of the world where earth and sky meet.

He paints himself red
And puts on a blanket of wolf-skin,
A feathered, rabbit-skin headdress.

He lights his pipe and points it to the sky.
He sings, and points his pipe to the earth.

He sings, and his canoe comes down like a cloud,
And carries him up across the sky.

MANDAN
Plains

NATALIA BELTING has occasionally found Indian artifacts on her own grounds in Urbana, Illinois. Miss Belting is an alumna of the University of Illinois and teaches in the school's history department. She has blended her historical scholarship with free-flowing poetic images to create other renowned books, including *The Land of the Taffeta Dawn* and *The Sun Is a Golden Earring*.

LASZLO KUBINYI studied at the Boston Museum School and at the School of Visual Arts in New York City, where he and his wife now live. Mr. Kubinyi has illustrated many children's books, including *Zeki and the Talking Cat Shukru* and *Haran's Journey*. Along with his artistic talent, Mr. Kubinyi is also a professional musician on the dumbek, a Middle Eastern drum.

The text type was set in Palatino and the display type in Hadriano Stone Cut and Palatino. The book was printed by offset.